Rivers From a Poet's Heart

By

Mikaela Hinterberger

For everyone, everywhere, who has finally learned what I have — to be raw when all I want to do is hide

Adulthood

I see it on the paper,
"legal adult"
But I spent my twenty-first birthday
Coloring and watching Winnie the Pooh
And now, the days are a blur
With most of my wants revolving around
How I want to see my mother
How I want to hang out with my dad
How I want to sing for my grandma
How I want to hold children
How I want to laugh

I cried last night because I am not
Who I wanted to be.
But I spent tonight
Drinking and coloring with crayons.

Wonder

I don't look for you anymore,
I don't search for an unfamiliar form;
Because now I know your face,
The curve of your neck,
Your lilting step and confident stance.
No longer do I wonder if I'll like your laugh,
Or the way you brush your teeth;
Now I'll just stand and watch,
Because I adore your every move.

Tiptoe

You tiptoed in

Silent feet on the carpet of my heart

You tidied up and swept the floor

And cooked me breakfast too

You took a needle and some thread

To mend the holes I couldn't see

You threw back the curtains that hid my pain

Coaxing it to come out and live

You opened windows to let in sun

A joy I hadn't seen

You transformed a hovel into a home

With your words, your thoughts, and your deeds

Deep Talks, Shattered Dreams

I stood up straight and tall and proud,
Pretending those words didn't pierce
My cold shell that I imagined I had

But as I stood there and watched her mouth
Tell me all the things I hoped I'd never hear
My heart crumbled, but first shattered with the blows

Inwardly I'm on my knees with tears streaming down and I can't breathe
But I'm standing here and I look okay
With marble for a face and granite for a heart

When she's done, I quietly nod and walk majestically from the room
I close my door and numb, collapse;
I stare at the wall as she resumes her life.

Biased

I sit and play a mournful song
On Sorrow and what it's like to live it
The strange part is that my heart remembers
But my soul is full of you

It forgot the pain of waking up
With dark thoughts of forever alone
It forgot how much a word can hurt
When it's angled in barbaric ways

Instead it sees your face and smile
The encouraging words you say
It remembers every moment of you
In a perfect, biased way

Potatoes

I love you more than I love potatoes
Which is a lot because potatoes are the most delicious thing on this planet
But you're kind of like them
Because I like them baked or mashed or as chips or boiled or in salad or in soup or fried
I get them any way I want them
And you?
You say I can have you any way I want you
Which is kind of perfect because I want you in every way
I want you in bed or out of bed or in the shower or in the kitchen while you cook potatoes
So it ends up being perfect
I love you
I love potatoes
But you will always win over the potatoes
And if there was a potato famine, I would live
But if there was a famine from you, I would probably die
Unless I had potatoes to console me
But even then, I doubt I'd live
And that's saying a lot because I'm Irish
And potatoes are pretty much the staple of my life
Therefore.
You beating out potatoes is kind of a big deal
Basically, I love you
And nothing
Even potatoes
Can change that

Never Clean Enough

The sunshine shone across my floor so clean
Lemon-Brite, sparkling white in the daytime;
Brilliant light casting a shimmering sheen,
I smiled at what had been covered in grime.

Clouds roll in and the thunder threatens me
Rain pours down, making puddles on the ground.
Willing it to leave, in a silent plea,
My heart sinks low as I hear a loud sound.

The kids clomp inside with their dirty feet,
Muddy grey attacks my floor, thickly spread;
I stand and stare, muted in my defeat.
What once was clean is now gritty and slick.

Why can I never have things my own way?
I sigh as I pick up my cleaning spray.

Melody

You are the melody that never leaves my head
My feet dance along without my knowledge
The words are on my tongue with every breath
And my heart knows every line

"Where did this song come from?"
My fuzzy brain cries out
"Why didn't we hear it sooner?"
My soul pipes in

Entranced, my body follows your lead
Each note reverberating through every inch of me
Sometimes we're in fields of flowers
Sometimes in lonely deserts

Hauntingly at times, I hear your melody
And my hands reach for a form they cannot see
Joyfully at times, I sing in harmony
As you clasp me tightly and I lean into you

You are the only melody I want to hear
And the only harmony I want to sing
You are my rock and my love
And I'm alive when I'm with you

Exist

If I had known you existed
I'd have gone to my doctor's visits
I'd have learned to play guitar
And how to sing like you do.

Had I known you existed
I'd have never wasted my time
With men who only saw my body
And didn't care to see my soul.

When I knew that you existed
My heart reared up its head
A throbbing flowed into my veins
Through a heart that newly felt

Now I know that you exist
And I'm never going back;
I'll be the best that I can be
Because your love challenges every part of me.

If

If words were woven craftily
And tongues could form them sweet
Then I would always have a way
Of telling you my love

If voices sang as mockingbirds
And each note was purely joy
Then I would always have a way
Of singing you my love

If actions were like building house
And all the bricks were trust
Then I would always have a way
Of showing you my love

If movement flowed as ecstasy
And each breath came with a beat
Then I would always have a way
Of dancing you my love

Oh and if my heart was not a stone
And the leaded weight would lift
Then I might find a way
Of saying that we're through

You

Your arms are my stronghold
Your lips my very warmth
Your eyes are the crawling ivy
That crumbles down my walls

Your voice is my sanity
Your laughter is my life
Your fingers are the lifelines
That hold me when I fall

Every single part of me is attached to who you are
And I never want to be apart
Not ever
Not at all

Better

I reminisce on what we had,
Of who we used to be
And chuckle now at who we are,
How much more you mean to me.

You are my moon and my stars,
My earth stops when you're away
Each ray of sun is from your dazzling smile,
And my life is better this way.

Nightmares

See her there as she's strapped to a chair, as she trembles like a leaf and can't speak. The inner thoughts of a raging mind, she spirals so deep she cannot come back. Shake and sweat and scream and strain, but nothing has she to cure the pain. It's a struggle, it's a battle, it's a mountain, it's a scar; it's the part of her like us that makes us who we are. Nobody cares that her mind is a mess and she shakes and she screams and she's left in the dark. She chokes as she lets out her one final breath, only to wake up to the things she has left. And she sways as she stands and falls to the floor, her hands weakly grasping the things that seem real. With a start! Then she sees that the things that were real were only the things of a minds' fairy tale. Here she is now with a lamp on a shelf and a shirt on the floor, a bed sheet that's drenched in the cold sweat of turmoil. She looks and she thinks and she shakes like a leaf; she looks and she breathes and tries to feel relief. All she can feel is the fear and her eyes open wide; she cannot go back to that dark place inside. Don't make me go back to that dark place inside. "Don't make me go back", her strangled heart cries, as her eyes grow tired and she fights with what's left. "I can't do it, I won't. I don't have the strength"; over and over until she's lulled into sleep. And now they're coming again as she dizzily fights, a losing battle that wages only at night.

Dad

One look in the mirror and
You see broken, you see marred
You see fragments of the man
You think is who you are

But I see the same reflection
As I'm looking from above
And the only thing staring back at me
Is pure and perfect love

You have been my rock
And you have been my endless ocean
Full of love, peace and devotion
You taught me to feel every emotion

Your friendship is a precious gift
The best you ever gave
You forgive me time and time again
When I see nothing left to save

Your wise words give me the chance
To mess up or to hear
How much you love me even when
I don't want to care

You raise me from my broken state
And gently fix my scars
There's nothing that I have done
To deserve the man you are

I love each moment spent with you
Whether joyful or in pain
In some really twisted way
Your love has kept me sane

Afternoon Echoes

Afternoon echoes as the sun bounces 'round
Rays that spill through the windows and tumble to the floor
Laughing playfully, they scramble like puppies and
Create new rainbows through dusty old glass

Afternoon echoes with the throb of nature's pulse
Every sound a breath, every sight a sigh
Light twists back and forth and dances to the beat
Lub-dub, lub-dub, she sways rhythmically in time

Afternoon echoes for the man with the stethoscope
He listens so closely and translates the sound
Sunshine beams in, making x-rays glow bright
She entwines her arms with the technician in white

That Extra Hour

This time change is screwing with me
I slipped the clock an hour behind
It's supposed to be great, supposed to be nice
That extra hour.
But now I lie here, sleepless and alone
Counting the ticks and the tocks
Daydreaming of the day you return
And I curse that extra hour.

Doubt

I never thought elevators would make me claustrophobic, but then you were gone and I couldn't breathe

Steel walls, steel doors, steel like your heart, like you steal my heart

Steel, steal, stole

Stomped on

Ruined

Thrown away.

You left me in a corner and crumpled my very being.

Any ounce of life was gone with your smile

Every desire to be better, wandered out with your eyes.

The thought of starting again?

Knives in my stomach

Moving my hand to wipe my tears?

Useless. I shouldn't bother; each drop is replaced by a brother, a sister, an aunt.

Trapped in a waterfall of madness, I sink slowly.

My brain can't comprehend what it is you've just done;

You've taken my life, my love, my thoughts

And you've left me with the memories;

You could have at least been decent enough to take those with you.

I don't want to remember, I want to be numb

I don't want to picture you in the drizzling rain, under that ratty umbrella you love,

I don't want to see the way you throw your head back when you're laughing at me,

I don't want to recreate that time you cooked dinner and the smoke alarm went off,

I don't want to remember how you looked on one knee.

Why couldn't you take your goddamn memories?
You left me with
Every.
Single.
One.
And the pain sears through my soul, like the branding iron on my heart
I've tried to stand, to be strong and independent like you always said I was
But maybe I'm not.
Because you said you'd always be here
And now you're not.
So maybe you just glibly made things up,
Maybe you never believed them at all
Maybe I'm not really beautiful and maybe my eyes don't really sparkle,
Maybe I'm not a good writer and maybe you never liked the way I danced,
Maybe you never thought we'd actually work out and maybe you were scared to give me your last name.
Did it ever occur to you that with every step towards that door, and with every unexplained moment,
I'd be led here, doubting.
Doubting myself because you aren't here to back me up,
Doubting what's real because you promised this would never happen,
So it must not be real.
But it is.
And I still don't know how.

Found

I have found the one I want to hold
I'll hold him now while I am young
And I'll hold him close when we are old
Each moment brings me closer to his heart
No one else will make me change my mind
He and I
Never apart

Mess

How lucky I am to be sorrowful and moody!
How amazing it is to have a reason to be sad!
I have you and I know what joy you bring to me
And I'm a mess when you're away.

But how fantastic it is to feel my heart hurt!
How thrilling to feel the throbbing in my veins!
How ecstatic I am to taste salty tears
And how thankful I am to know what I'm missing

I have you and I know the love we share
And I'm a mess when you're away.

Light

Rocking, washing, back and forth,
All those things I cannot see,
Blind in this dazzling darkness,
Yet eyes look for a key.

The pain put off until its time,
The darkness all for now -
Dazed and Numb may capture me;
The Light will come, but how?

A ring of endless Light
Much purer than the air,
Brings me to my knees
And makes me welcome there.

Gently He extends His arms,
The splendor of His love,
Spreading hope and life to me
And raising me above.

The darkness now so stark and bare,
Not dazzling nor so bright,
My eyes are opened once again
To His ring of endless Light.

White Pages

I sit and I see white surrounding me. White pages ripped out, white pages stained black with ink. Ink that will darken my wrists as I slump to the desk because my head is too heavy to hold. A twitch as I rise to rub the sleep from my eyes because I have too much to do, too much to write, too much ink to smear across the white canvas of what needs to turn into something passable. Something that needs to be graded with an A. Something that I can look at and know that I did okay. That the scratches that rent my paper in two suddenly transformed and became something new. I grumble because it's never perfect, because what I want to say never looks right; but I sigh and I switch off the light because in the dark of night, it's all the same as one black page.

Breakfast

You woke up hungry
Which is new for you
So I found some Breakfast
Which you actually ate
You fell back asleep pretty quick
But only slept for an hour when
I woke you up because
I had a nightmare again
You held me and told me to feed it hay
(Apparently mares are just hungry)
Speaking of, you were ready for food;
Second Breakfast is now your thing
I called you a Hobbit
When you asked for elevensies
And laughed when you wanted brunch
Prednisone will do that to you
I said with a wink
But the reality is,
Breakfast became your favorite meal

I didn't

I'd like to say I didn't cry

That I didn't turn out the lights

And sit alone in the dark

I'd like to say that I was strong

That life was normal

And I moved on

But I admit, I played sad songs

And Annie sang along

I went to bed early so that

I could sleep my way through the hours

So I could focus on everything but you

I woke up to you, everywhere I looked

Cologne on my dresser, a picture on my wall

A toothbrush in the bathroom, a flight number on my table

I almost wished those things away because it hurt to miss you that much

But I left them to remind me of the time you were coming home

Dirt

I went for a walk on a breezy day
The sun shone, lightly filtered through the pines
I stood still and breathed the mint
I'd crushed beneath my feet

I went for a walk on a rainy day
The tiny footfalls of rain, soaking through my shirt
I turned up my face and drank it deep
As I'd done for years

I went for a walk on a tired day
The sky was bleak and close, with Atlas asking to rest
I searched for a flower to pick
Like I'd always done on tired days

I went for a walk on a dusty day
Poofs of reddish brown, mushrooming in clouds as I stepped
I tried to stay clean
But I'd never get the dirt from these clothes.

No, I'd never get the dirt from these clothes.

Imagine

Lying here alone, I imagine things

I imagine how you'll look when you step off your plane,

Clothes wrinkled, eyes sleepy, beard stubble going strong.

I imagine how your pace picks up, quicker and quicker,

As you walk towards where I'm waiting.

I imagine your face light up when your eyes find me

And I imagine your suitcase chasing you as you rush into my universe

I imagine your arms enfolding me and my head cuddled into your neck

I imagine your smell and the way your arms protect me from the world

I imagine the words you'll whisper in my ear;

The "I love yous", "I missed yous", the "I'm so glad you're heres".

I imagine the airport melting away

As our mouths find each other for the first time in years

I imagine our night home, when you finally lock our door

I imagine you taking my shoes off and throwing my socks on the floor

I imagine your hands running up and down my legs

I imagine your lips on my thighs, my stomach, my breasts;

I imagine my hands exploring your body

I imagine the journeys we'll take in one night

I imagine these things

But most of all,

I like to imagine you're imagining them too.

Anthill

Loving you is like living in an anthill
Chaotic, scrambling, rushing, always in a frenzy
Somehow it's organized, somehow it's rational
Somehow it's comfortable, somehow it's home

Me

I take care
Of children with their grubby fingers
Of animals with their wagging tails
Of plants with their reaching leaves
Of dishes with their unfinished meals
Of adults with their angry words
Of boyfriends with their many needs

But never me.

Shall I Compare Thee to a White Refrigerator?

You are my refrigerator, running constantly

Full of things I need for life

Offering all you have

You hold the things I love the most

The perfect size for what I need;

You are there in the dark and shed new light

The perfect comfort when things are going wrong,

Knowing what I'm searching for.

But there are times when you fail me

And I come to find you pale and empty,

Then it's my turn to take care of you;

I bring you things to fill you up

When you lack the luster to make me smile.

Eventually I'll lean against you and you'll hold me up

You lovingly support me when I'm too tipsy to stand

You never laugh or judge when I ask you for a beer

You listen with a pleasant hum that soothes and makes me calm

You notice the men I bring home because they always meet you in the morning

But you're kind to them and never say anything rude

You silently stand and patiently wait for me to realize you've always been there

At times I forget because I'm busy with life but

I starve without your presence.

With You

There is not a part of me
That is the same as when we met
Tainted with a precious love
I'm better than the woman I was

I had long since given up,
True love was not for me
Silently you wandered in
And now I doubt myself

I doubt that I can live alone
Without your voice or laugh
I doubt that I still want my last name
When yours sounds so pleasant on my lips

I doubt that I'll feel beautiful
Without you saying so
I doubt that I will ever be
The way that I once was

The best thing of all
Is that I never want to go back
To being the person who meandered nowhere.
All I want now is to meander

Somewhere
Nowhere
Everywhere
With you.

Maybe

On the edge of tears, not giving in
I put it off but it rises until it overflows
Ebb and flow, ebb and flow, I was fine but now I crumble
Falling fast to the deep and dark
I asked the nurse but she can't heal a heart
I stumble along, eyes dazed and red, pushing forward to escape the night
Nothing works and my breath comes quick
My throat contracts and my hands cover my mouth
Stifle the sound, stifle the hurt, if they can't hear it, they can't tell
Sink in a corner, body shakes ready to fall in pieces
I put it off, but one small crack, I'm lost again in the shards that composed my being
Pick up my head, glance around; nobody notices turmoil when they themselves are hurting
Nobody notices one heart when theirs is already too heavy
Just like before, again and again, a distress signal is issued with no response.
Nobody hears and nobody cares; it's too hard to live with an extra burden
I push wearily to my feet; I stand, grasp the wall, fingers slip
Pain. That's new. Physical pain rips through.
Through my fingers, through my arm, shivering delightedly as it meets my heart.
Too cold, too numb to care. The blood is not a part of me; I see it and I turn to walk.
Left, right, left, right, foot catches on a brick. Tumble down, don't care.
Left limp, right; wander through ceaseless night.
Here I remain, I tread up rocky terrain; up and up I trudge along
Maybe one day I'll complete the song
Maybe one day I'll stand up tall, erase what I feel and rule my all
Maybe one day I'll be able to see that the only thing I'm fighting is me.

I love you

It was a little Dutch shoe that my grandfather had,
It sat on his shelf looking happy in its bright red.
I remember always liking it because it never changed;
Always the same spot, off on the left with a little bit of dust.
I'd ask about the shoe, that little Dutch creation,
Grandpa would reply with a story as long as he was tall;
He'd sit me down and say, "Well, mein fraulein, let me tell you about it."
And every time he told it, I waited for the end;
I didn't wait because I wanted him to stop talking,
I waited because his last words were always my favorites.
"Ich liebe dich", he'd say with a smile
A big rough Army man with his big rough words,
But it was the sweetest sound to me.

Home

Home is feet running to meet you
The sparkle of a child's eye
A moment of bliss

Home is the innocent laughter
The precious tears
A memory of a night

Home is a word whispered in your ear
The little hands to hold
A dance seen by the King

Home is the reckless abandon
The stillness of sleep
A song unknown to the world

Home is muddled confusion
The emergencies of life
A need for patience

Home is a tall tree
The sharp blade of green
A hope in the dark

Home is a gift undeserved
The heartbeat of an age
A second chance

Home is a glowing warmth
The unending forgiveness
A Sovereign love

Home is rags in a stable
The cry of my Messiah
A Light for this world

Home is the precious Savior
The Son on a cross of wood
A lifetime of sin crucified

Home is so simple
The touch of grace
A heart thawed once again

Home is a soul at rest
A joyful thought of Heaven
A place to spend eternity

Home is with You
The one place I belong
A perfect ending

The Haze

A smoky haze, cough clears a path, blinkers loud on a dark night. Stop at the light and watch it blink from red to green to a yellowish hue, not really sure who we are or what do to. We waste our days in a cubicle, behind a counter, waiting for a chance to be better, but then we take that chance and run like the wind. We run far away and we never know where we go or what we do or why we even do what we do. Then we get stuck wishing we were different but too lazy to figure out why we stay the same. We live for summer nights when we can roll down the windows and scream out the frustration where no one can hear as Def Leppard deafens the din of our everyday life. And we wonder why it's not enough, why we're stale, pale, and utterly unworthy. We blame it on the drugs, the binge drinking, the studying we should have done, the studying we did; it never occurs to us that maybe our parents fucked up but that we don't have to be that way. Why do we accept defeat before we've even begun to fight? We gladly take the weak when it would only take a bit of effort to be strong. We are the problem. We are the solution. We are everything and that makes us helpless. We start to see what we could be and we shy away because it's, "only me". Gotta love working with the lie, the lie that destroys you from the inside out because it takes your pride, it takes your will, it takes your effort, it takes your desires, it takes your fight. Stand and fight. No longer accept defeat. If you accept defeat, just accept death instead; it's certainly less humiliating.

Cello

A body so beautifully carved

Only melodies could come from it

I rest my fingers on her neck

So perfect

No flaws

I know her better than I know myself

She consumes me

She took my soul and transformed it

She changed my very essence with her presence

My hands gently hold her

My legs support her

She speaks how I feel

And I feel as she speaks

Blues Inspiration

He slipped his arm around me and twirled me so my skirt stood out like a newly opened morning glory. Each step was perfectly timed and as the slow jazz led us on the dance floor, my feet forgot they were my own. They became the floor, they became one with the music, with their partner, with the aromatic atmosphere. The ballroom seemed to hold no one except the slow, steady beat, and his soul. He led as though we were dancing on air; his hand gently telling me which way to turn, his body indicating the ease with which he led. His eyes found nothing in the room except my face, and everything else faded as we looked into eternity.

Made in the USA
Charleston, SC
12 March 2016